LOST TREASURES:

THE WOODEN SYNAGOGUES

OF EASTERN EUROPE

ARTWORK AND TEXT BY
BILL FARRAN

LOST TREASURES:

THE WOODEN SYNAGOGUES

OF EASTERN EUROPE

ARTWORK AND TEXT BY
BILL FARRAN

Dedication

Three Menches (men) on a Bench

This book is dedicated to the people who prayed in Eastern Europe's Wooden Synagogues, and to those of us who wish they were still here.

Table of Contents

The Jews of Eastern Europe: A Brief History

There has been a Jewish presence in Poland for over one thousand years. The first mention of Jews in Poland was reported by a Spanish Jewish merchant, Ibrahim Ibn Jacob, in the year 966. By 1264 there were so many Jewish settlements that Duke Bolesław the Pious, granted Jews on his land the Statute of Kalisz, enumerating their rights and obligations, lasting until the decline of the First Commonwealth.

The Polish-Lithuanian Commonwealth became a place of refuge and home to the world's largest Jewish community at a time when Jews were persecuted and expelled from various Western European countries. In addition to forced expulsions, among the contributing factors to Jewish migration were the increased antisemitic feelings during the Crusades, the BlackPlague, the Catholic Church's desire to convert Jews, Christian guilds wanting to limit competition, and kings and princes wishing to be free of their debt to Jewish bankers.

Thus, the Polish-Lithuanian Commonwealth was the most welcoming and tolerant country in Europe for the Jewish people. So much so that it was referred to by historians as *paradisus judaeorum* ("Paradise of the Jews"). Jews were invited to settle on the Commonwealth's private estates, which were large tracts of land, owned by the Polish nobility. Jews were valued because they were literate, multi-lingual, and possessed business skills. They were able to turn rural settlements into thriving market towns **(shtetls)** that provided great wealth for the noble landowners.

The shtetl was a unique type of market town, requiring three elements: land owned by Polish Catholic noblemen, the Polish, Belorussian, the Ukrainian and Lithuanian serfs who lived on and worked the land, and the Jews who managed the absentee noble's estate, collecting rents and taxes from the serfs and operating the nobles' taverns and distilleries, which provided the greatest source of income for many noblemen.

Serfs were in perpetual debt, as the nobleman claimed an exorbitant part of their crops and required them to buy seed, rent animals, tools and the hovels in which they lived.

The shtetl's Jews held leases (the Arenda System) from the nobility to run taverns, flour mills, lumber industries, cattle, engage in horse trading and breeding, grain processing and shipping and the many jobs needed to be done in a small town. On weekly market days, serfs came to town to attend church, have a drink, sell their surplus products as well as to buy goods and services from the Jews.

The decline of the shtetl's Golden Age began with the Partition of Poland, when Prussia, Austria-Hungary and Russia divided Poland, destroying the Polish nobility and with it, Jewish prosperity. Later, Jews became victims of the fighting on the Eastern Front of World War I where many lived, followed by the Holocaust which was responsible for the near-total destruction of European Jewry.

Shtetl Names

Every shtetl had various names using Latin, Cyrillic, and Hebrew alphabets, according to the residing ethnic population. Nobles and peasants used names and alphabets of their native language, while Jews used Yiddish or Hebrew. The governing Russian, German and Austrian authorities used Russian, or German place names. This book will use town names of their current nation and mention their Yiddish and Polish names.

Living in the Shadow of the Tsar

Wooden Synagogues

The wooden synagogue style developed between the mid-sixteenth to mid-seventeenth centuries, a time often referred to as the "*Golden Age of Polish Jewry*." It was a period of peace and prosperity for the Jews of modern-day Lithuania, Poland, Belarus, and Ukraine during the time when they were residents of the vast former Polish-Lithuanian Commonwealth.

More than one thousand synagogues were built, of which 180 are considered valuable and historically important. They incorporated many of the features of the Baroque style. Most notable, however, were the elaborate wall paintings found in many of these wooden synagogues, transforming space from the ordinary to the glorious. Synagogue art brought together the essence of the Torah, everyday images from the lives of the shtetl dwellers, Jewish mysticism, accurate and imagined visions of Jerusalem, in combination with regional architectural design reflecting European style and local artistic traditions.

The synagogues fulfilled both religious and social roles in the lives of the Jewish communities. They were places for prayer, for discussion of matters affecting the community, judging the guilty, teaching and for study of the Torah. The building faced east, and the other buildings of the Jewish community surrounded the synagogue. Only the eastern wall, in accordance with the directives of the Talmud, remained free of outbuildings.

Before World War II, a few wooden synagogues were victims of old age, fire, and war. The remaining vast majority were destroyed by the Nazis who attempted to wipe out Eastern European's Jewish population and to destroy the monuments of Jewish culture. A handful have survived in Lithuania and Ukraine, where they are falling to ruin due to neglect.

Two full scale replicas of wooden synagogues have been built in southeastern Poland. The Polaniec synagogue is in the *Open-Air Ethnographic Museum* in Sandok and the Volpa synagogue is in Bilgoraj.

Introduction by Dr. Tomasz Wisniewski

Historian, Author and Film Maker

At one time, the Polish-Lithuanian Commonwealth was the largest European nation, including most of today's Poland, Ukraine, Estonia, and all of Belarus, Lithuania, and Latvia. Because the area was heavily forested, wood was the cheapest building material. Simple homes were built from logs, as were massive buildings that served as manor houses, town halls, taverns, inns, churches, and synagogues.

It was within the Commonwealth that wooden synagogues were constructed, and they have been a source of fascination due to their unique beauty and style. The spellbound included architects, historians, and artists as well as people who prayed within the synagogues. Maria and Kazimierz Piechotka, experts in the architecture of wooden synagogues, wrote: "The spatial sophistication of these synagogues and the very high level of structural solutions allow us to look for their creators among the most outstanding artists of the era."

I, too, was infatuated with wooden synagogues. In my book, *"Synagogues and Jewish Communities in the Bialystok Region: Jewish life in Eastern Europe Before 1939"*, I devoted a large segment to the wooden synagogues of the Bialystok region. To do so, I researched and analyzed archival photos, old drawings, paintings, and etchings which were such a delight that I could not take my eyes off the images, especially the photographs. I ordered prints from the archives at maximum resolution, just to be able to taste the richness and beauty of the buildings. My research was limited to a small area, while Bill Farran researched the entire Commonwealth of Poland and Lithuania.

Two artists, from dissimilar parts of the world and different generations, American Bill Farran and Bialystoker (Poland) Moishe Verbin, were so enchanted with wooden synagogues that they each created series of artworks to depict the structures. Verbin created wood and straw models, while Farran created wood and linocut prints. Similarly, they both began their journey with gifts created for loved ones: Bill made a Mother's Day wood print and Moishe wove a Star of David for his wife.

Bill was taught to love all things made of wood by his carpenter grandfather and was enthralled by stories about the family in Europe told by his grandmother as she helped Bill with his Yiddish school homework.

A multifaceted passion, an interest in geography, architecture, culture, and art closely linked to defining his own heritage gave Farran's work a deeper and more thoughtful meaning. This natural motivation was compounded by a desire to understand his own heritage: his ancestors hailed from Belarus, Latvia, Ukraine, while his wife's roots were in Poland and Lithuania, areas where hundreds of

6

wooden synagogues dotted the landscape. It is within these contexts that it is easy to understand why, for Bill, the phenomenon of wooden synagogues evoked nostalgia, and a creative restlessness of trying to restore the memory of these objects. This emotion, combined with amazement, is undoubtedly what he succumbed to.

Thus, it seems natural that as he created artworks of wooden synagogues, he would study the history of wooden synagogues, the towns where they were built, and the history and culture of the people who attended these synagogues becoming an expert in their history.

In 2013, Bill Farran and his wife Elaine came to Europe, visiting Lithuania, Belarus, and Poland to trace their roots. While in the small town of Michalow (near Bialystok) he managed to do something more. There, at the Film, Sound and Photography Studio, I organized a unique event, featuring an exhibition of Bill's linocuts, which we called "The Days of Jewish Culture." Bill gave a fascinating lecture, illustrated by his linocuts, followed by a klezmer group singing Yiddish songs, a lecture by the last living Jewish resident of Bialystok, Zbigniew Siwiński, a lesson in making felafel, and samplings of traditional Jewish foods.

So now, Bill Farran's wonderful book of wooden synagogues has been published. We wanted so much for its premiere to take place in Poland, here in Bialystok. We had planned to present an art show, and provide a workshop on linocut technique, but the Covid 19 pandemic and the terrible war in Ukraine thwarted these plans.

Thanks to Bill Farran's linocuts, Moshe Verbin's models and the archival photos on which these works of art are based, the beautiful wooden synagogues and their unique architecture can be studied and brought back to life, if only for a moment.

Tomasz Wisniewski

www.bagnowka.com

POLAND

Torah Ark (Aron Kodesh

**Bakałarzewo ~ Gabin ~ Janow Sokolski
Jedwabne ~ Końskie ~ Kórnik ~ Kosow Lacki
Lipsko ~ Lutomiersk ~ Mogielnica ~ Nasielsk
Nowe Maistro ~ Piaski ~ Połanicc
Przedbórz ~ Rakow ~ Sidra ~ Sierpc ~ Sobkow
Wasilkow ~ Wyszokie Mazowiecki ~ Zabłudów**

Bakałarzewo, Poland
Yiddish: Baklerove

The Old Cold Shul, Behind the Beit Midrash

Bakałarzewo, once part of the Polish-Lithuanian Commonwealth, is a village in Poland, set among dense forests, beautiful hills, and rivers. According to 17th century Parish Chronicles, the town's name was derived from a bachelor who once lived there. Bakałarzewo became an active town with the arrival of merchants and the establishment of trade during the mid-1700's, with a Jewish population settling around 1670.

By the 19th century, more than threequarters of the town's population was Jewish and a wooden synagogue was constructed during 1849.

In 1870, Russian authorities reduced Bakałarzewo to the status of a village as a punishment for the town's participation in the January Uprising. No longer able to hold fairs, a massive portion of income was lost. The assassination of Tsar Alexander II in March 1881 resulted in state sponsored pogroms against Jews and many of the town's Jews emigrated to the United States or larger towns.

The town suffered great hardship during World War I, when Bakałarzewo was devastated. Again, Jews fled, although some chose to return later. Many found their homes destroyed but were determined to rebuild their lives.

By 1939, however, most of Bakałarzewo's Jews had left the town, realizing their proximity to Germany presented great danger. Their assumption was correct as the town was burned down by German bombs on the first day of Worl War II.

Gąbin, Poland
Yiddish: Gombin

The wooden synagogue of Gabin was built in 1710. The facade of the synagogue was inspired by the Baroque architecture of churches. Built as a timber-framed rectangle, it was ornamented with two onion-shaped domed towers over the entrance, each with a flag. In more modern times, the synagogue was regarded as a landmark historical building, part of the national cultural heritage under special supervision of the Department of Museums of the Polish Ministry of Education.

On September 21, 1939, the Jewish population of Gąbin was gathered in the market by the German Nazis, who brutalized and killed many. On that same day, the soldiers set the synagogue on fire, spreading to nearby buildings. The fire consumed the Torah, the prayer books, and all synagogue equipment. Several Jews in the burning building miraculously escaped death. In the end, the Germans blamed the Jews for starting the fire.

Janow Sokolski, Poland

Yiddish: Yanov

Janow Sokolski was a small town in the Bialystok region. Jews began to settle in Janow as early as the 17th century. In 1719 the Bishop of Vilno, Konstanty Brzostowski, granted them permission to build a synagogue, which was constructed in 1740.

The town's census in 1775 counted 214 Christian residents and 221 Jews. In 1897, of the town's 2,296 residents, 1,797 were Jewish. Just prior to World War II, nearly 1,100 Jews lived in this small, poor town known for its hotel, which was owned by Jewish resident Chmiel Rudawski.

The wooden synagogue was one of the most impressive in the region with a monumental three-storyroof. It was renovated and maintained by the Polish State Office for Historical Buildings. The Jewish community and its wooden synagogue perished at the hands of the Nazis.

Jedwabne, Poland
Yiddish: Yedvavna

Jedwabne is a small town in the Bialystok region of Poland. The Polish nobleman who owned the town invited Jews to settle there. By the 18th Century Jedwabne received rights to hold local fairs on Sunday and five country fairs a year. Their large wooden synagogue was built in 1770.

On July 10, 1941, while the German SS stood by, Mayor Marian Karolak led a group of Polish men from Jedwabne to round up the Jews, forcing them into the town square. After being brutalized and beaten, many were killed. Later that day most of the remaining three hundred Jews were led to a barn, locked inside, and burned alive. This pogrom was conducted by the Polish citizens of Jedwabne.

Knowledge of the massacre only became widespread in 1999–2003 due to the work of Polish filmmakers, journalists, and academics, in particular Jan Gross's 2001 work *"Neighbors: The Destruction of the Jewish Community in Jedwabne, Poland"*. Public interest in the incident prompted a forensic murder investigation in 2000–2003 by Poland's Institute of National Remembrance, which confirmed that the direct perpetrators were ethnic Poles. The country was shocked by the findings, which challenged common narratives about the Holocaust in Poland that focused on Polish suffering and heroism, and that non-Jewish Poles had little responsibility for the fate of Poland's Jews.

Końskie, Poland
Yiddish: Kinsk

Końskie was founded as a town in 1748. Jewish residents began to settle there before that time, as the first written mention of Jews dates to 1588. By the second half of the 18th century, attesting to the community's growth, one of Poland's first large synagogues was erected in 1780 at the invitation of King John III Sobieski. By this time, the Końskie community had its own cemetery, Chevra Kadisha (group of volunteers on call to prepare a deceased person for burial according to Jewish traditions), as well as other communal institutions.

The Końskie synagogue was a large, wooden structure noted for its architectural style, and is classified as one of the most unique examples of wooden synagogue architecture in Poland. Equally impressive was the synagogue's interior, with a stunning bimah located in the center of the building.

The Końskie Jewish community enjoyed its magnificent synagogue until the outbreak of World War II. On the evening of September 11, 1939, the synagogue was burned to the ground by the German occupying authorities soon after their conquest of the town.

Końskie Bimah

14

Kórnik, Poland
Yiddish: Kurnik

Jewish people first settled in the small town of Kórnik in the Poznan province during the early 17th century.

The town's wooden synagogue was constructed in 1767 by Hillel Benjamin of Lasko. It was built in the classical Tuscan style, which was common to the local manor houses. The carved Torah Ark was older than the structure and was brought over from another synagogue. The ceiling and the walls were covered with colorful paintings, as was typical of wooden synagogues.

Kórnik became part of Prussia after the Partition of Poland. The largest recorded Jewish population of Kórnik was in 1840 when 1,170 Jews made up 43 percent of the population. Kórnik experienced a steady decline in Jewish population as Jews moved to larger cities in Germany, Europe, and America.

By 1939 there were only 36 Jews remaining in Kórnik. The synagogue of Kórnik was burned down by the Germans during World War II.

Kosow Lacki, Poland
Yiddish: Kosov Latski

The wooden synagogue of Kosow Lacki, a town whose majority was Jewish, was erected at the end of the 18th century. Unlike other synagogues, Kosów Lacki's was not known for its architectural structure, nor for its interior paintings. It is remembered instead for the ironic and tragic ending of its Jewish inhabitants.

Between the two World Wars, many Jews began to leave Kosow Lacki as their situation worsened with the rise of Hitler and conflict in the area between Germans and Russians. Thus, the Jewish population dwindled to 40% of the town's population by the start of World War II. In late September 1939, the Germans occupied the town, established a Judenrat and ghetto. Jewish craftsmen became slave labor, some working to erect and enlarge nearby Treblinka from a small POW camp into a death camp.

At the end of Yom Kippur on September 22, 1942, German and Polish police circled the ghetto and, on the same day, marched its inhabitants six miles to Treblinka. They were the only victims to arrive on foot to this death camp.

Lipsko, Poland
Yiddish: Lipsk

The town of Lipsko belonged to the Krepski, Deenhoff, Sanguszek and Kochanowski Polish families. In 1662, 497 Christians and 22 Jews paid a poll tax. The existence of a small Jewish settlement was registered in 1765 and a wooden synagogue was built the same year.

Since the reign of King Stanislaw August, who was the last King of the Polish-Lithuanian Commonwealth, the town was allowed to organize ten fairs and a weekly market on Sunday. The local population derived its income from agriculture, and the sale and distillation of alcohol. Following the final partition-of Poland, the town stagnated, with the population diminishing to less than one hundred people.

In 1868, as a punishment for residents' participation in the January Uprising, the Russians took away Lipsko's town rights, turning it into a village. This prohibited townspeople from holding fairs, decreasing everyone's income. During World War II, the German occupiers committed mass murders; among them was the event on September 8, 1939, when they burned alive sixty local Jews in the synagogue.

Lutomiersk, Poland

Yiddish: Lutomiersk

The noble family who owned Lutomiersk invited Jews to settle in the town in the 1600's. Sometime during the 1700's the town owners further encouraged Jewish enterprise by providing loans. By the middle of the 18th Century most of the town's population was Jewish. In addition to commercial trading, Jews were employed as shopkeepers, weavers, tanners, tailors, and carpenters. The Wooden Synagogue was built between 1763 and 1765 by Hillel Benjamin of Lasko* and destroyed during World War I.

In 1815 the Polish owners of Lutomiersk organized a home-based weaving industry. Jewish merchants supplied the weavers with raw materials and marketed their finish products, When Lodz became a major textile manufacturing city the population of nearby Lutomiersk declined as people moved to Lodz to seek employment.

Lutomiersk had a small Jewish population of 750 on the eve of World War II. Germans occupied the town in 1939 and it was incorporated directly into the Third Reich. The Germans authorities began a policy of exterminating the Jewish population and terrorizing the Polish population. The Lutomiersk ghetto was liquidated as its prisoners were brought to the Chelmo death camp at the end of July 1942.

*Hillel Bejamin of Laslo is known for being the architect and builder of the wooden synagogues of Lutomiersk, Kórnik and Zolochiv. After finishing the synagogue at Lutomiersk, he began construction of the wooden synagogue in Zolochiv. He died in a construction accident and is buried in Zolochiv.

Mogielnica, Poland
Yiddish: Mogelnitza

The first mention of Jews settling in Mogielnica was in 1777. By the middle of the 19th century most of the town was Jewish.

In 1828, Chaim Meir Jechiel Szapira, who was descended from an important Hasidic rabbinical family, established a yeshiva in the shtetl. His yeshiva attracted hundreds of Hasidic pilgrims into the town and in turn contributed to its economic development. In the mid-19th century, a beautiful wooden synagogue was constructed in Mogielnica.

During World War I, as the Russians were retreating from the advancing German Army, fearing that the Jews would be loyal to Germany, they expelled the entire Jewish population of five thousand Jews. After the war ended some Jews returned to Mogielnica.

The Germans seized Mogielnica on September 8, 1939. On the same day they burned down the wooden synagogue. In October 1939 they established the Judenrat which had to supply the Nazis with forced labor. On February 27 and 28, 1942, fifteen hundred Jews from Mogielnica were transported to the Warsaw Ghetto. There they were beaten, worked, and starved the death. Many were transported to the Treblinka Death Camp. On April 19, 1943, the Germans sent in tanks and heavy equipment to liquidate the Warsaw ghetto, The poorly armed Jews revolted and battled Germans until they were finally defeated on May 16, 1943.

Nasielsk, Poland

Yiddish: Nasielsk

Nasielsk, a town in east-central Poland in the Warszawa province, received its first municipal privileges in 1386. The Jewish community dates to the 16th century. By 1910 there were 4,742 Jews, representing 76% of the population. Jews thrived economically working in crafts and trade, and by working in a tannery and a plant that manufactured clothing and pearl buttons. Others participated in the town's economy as farmers and merchants. There were Jews who were wealthy or poor, and those who were secular or religious. However, their numbers dwindled to 2,691 by 1921 as economic hardship caused many to emigrate elsewhere.

The great Nasielsk synagogue was built in 1650 by Simcha Weiss, son of Shlomo of Luck. The first official inventory of important buildings in Poland, "*A General View of the Nature of Ancient Monuments in the Kingdom of Poland,*" led by Kazimierz Stronczynski, who describedthe Nasielsk Synagogue as one of Poland's architecturally notable buildings. The deteriorating synagogue was demolished in 1880 and replaced by a new brick one constructed on its site.

During World War II, the German Nazis murdered Nasielsk's Jewish citizens.

Nowe Miasto, Poland
Yiddish: Neishat

Nowe Miasto means new town. There are at least seven Nowe Miasto's in Poland. This Nowe Miasto is located at **52°39' N, 20°38' E**. The Jews did not face any obstacles in coming to settle in Nowe Miasto. In the second half of the 18th century, about 30 Jewish families lived in the town, who were occupied mainly in trades and commerce. A small group of Jewish merchants became wealthy from wholesale grain commerce and as leaseholders on plots of forest to be felled. In the late 19th century, Jews owned a water mill and a sawmill. The owner of the beer factory in Nowe Miasto was also a Jew. In these relatively large factories Jews were not employed, apart from family members of the owners and a few clerks.

In the mid-18th century, the Jews had an independent kehila [Jewish community council]. In this period, the old wooden synagogue was built, with artistic interior decoration, such as on the Torah ark and the bimah, carved from wood.

In the 1930s, the Jews of Nowe Miasto suffered greatly from the increasing anti-Semitism , then prevalent across Poland. Jewish peddlers were not permitted at all to enter the villages. On market days the Endeks [members of the anti-Semitic Polish Narodowa Demokracja party, placed boycott guards in front of Jewish shops and market stalls.

The Nazis occupied Nowe Miasto in late 1939. The Germans ordered the dismantling of the old synagogue, as they hesitated to burn it for fear of the fire spreading. In October of 1942, the Jewish town of Nowe Miasto ceased to exist.

Piaski, Poland

Yiddish: Piesk

The first Jews settled in Piaski as early as the seventeenth century. Their synagogue towered over the wooden houses of the town. Piaski was a typical shtetl inhabited by Jews with an intense sense of religious and traditional values.

In September 1939, Piaski was captured for a while by the Soviet Army marking the farthest point east of Lublin under their occupation. Soon after, the Soviets withdrew as part of the Molotov-Ribbentrop Pact, which enabled Soviet Russia and Nazi Germany to partition Poland between them. Piaski was the first town in Poland where the Nazis established a ghetto in the spring of 1940. Extreme overcrowding, hunger, disease, and slave labor plagued the ghetto Jews. Between March 1942 and November 1943, the ghetto was liquidated by sending the Jews to labor and death concentration camps.

The synagogue was destroyed during fighting between the Soviets and the Germans during World War II.

Połaniec, Poland
Yiddish: Plontch

In 1765, Jews were granted the privilege of residence in the town and permitted to open workshops. In the mid-18th century, the town had a synagogue, a Beit Midrash, a Talmud Torah, a Yeshiva, and many cheders. The synagogue was well known for its architecture and wall paintings.

A fire in 1929 swept through the town destroying the Beit Midrash, Mikvah and Talmud Torah, and leaving one hundred Jewish families homeless. The Jews rebuilt their homes using bricks and stones.

At the end of October 1942, the Polaniec ghetto was liquidated. Immediately after the deportation, the Nazis began to take over the abandoned properties and belongings. They destroyed the wooden houses and the newer stone houses were sold to enthusiastic Poles for token sums. Soon after, the Poles began intensive searches for hidden valuables within the buildings and courtyards.

The wooden synagogue, which had stood for five hundred years, was sold to the local Germans, who dismantled it and used it for firewood.

Przedborz, Poland

Yiddish: Pshedbosh

Przedborz was historically connected with the Polish Crown who contributed funds for the construction of its wooden synagogue, built after the previous synagogue burned down. Its date of completion was noted on a wall painting stating, *"This is the work of Yehuda Leib's own hands, 1760."*

Regarded by many as one of Poland's most beautiful wooden synagogues with distinctive features, it attracted tourists to the small town. Its exterior was modest, while its interior contained unique curved ceiling paneling along the single barrel vault with an intricate lunette and star motif that gave the impression of detailed carved latticework. The Baroque Torah Ark was elaborately carved with lions, flowers, and animals. Other elements included ornate Corinthian capitals on the pilasters, elaborate interior wall paintings, a menorah, an illustration of Psalm 137 with trees beside the river Babylon, musical instruments hanging from the branches, landscapes of towns and the texts of prayers surrounded by garlands of leaves with flowers.

The synagogue of Przedbórz was destroyed in 1939 by the Nazis.

Raków, Poland
Yiddish: Rakov

Raków was founded in 1567 by Jan Sienieński as a center for the Calvinist Polish Brethren. They advocated separation of church and state, taught equality, and brotherhood of all people, opposed social privileges based on religious affiliation, and their adherents refused military service. In the 1630's there were 15,000 people. However, the town's population dwindled to seven hundred when the Catholic rulers of Poland expelled the Polish Brethren in 1658.

Jews were a strong presence in the earliest history of the town since the establishment of a Jewish community in 1606. In 1663 the town had 977 residents, including 104 Jews, who were engaged in the sale of cloth and paper. The Raków wooden synagogue was built at the end of the 18th or beginning of the 19th century.

Raków experienced a population growth in the 19th century, reaching 1,232 people in 1827, among them 966 Jews, who were primarily engaged in trade and the sale of alcohol. By 1880, there were 1,979 people in the town, a majority of whom were Jewish.

The Jews of Raków were murdered by the Nazis and buried in a mass grave. In 1945 their remains were removed and reburied in Piotrkow in the Lodz region.

Sidra, Poland

Yiddish: Sidra

Sidra was a small town located in the Bialystok region of Poland, a region that was quite rural with an ethnically mixed population. The area had been inhabited for centuries by members of different nations and religions: Belarusians, Lithuanians, Ukrainians, Rusyns, Romanis, Tatars, and Jews. Religions consisted of Roman Catholics, Russian, Greek and Ukrainian Orthodox Christians, Muslims, and Jews who were Orthodox, Conservative, and Progressive.

The earliest known Jewish community was in the 17th century. The wooden synagogue was built by the end of the 18th or early 19th century. The main hall was square and was sunk three steps below the vestibule floor level, giving the synagogue a greater feeling of height. Synagogues could not be higher than the Church steeple of that town.

In 1921, the Jewish population consisted of 465 people. The Jewish town of Sidra was destroyed by the Nazis during World War II.

Sierpc, Poland

Yiddish name: Sheps, Sherpt

The earliest mention of a Jewish presence in the town dates to 1739. By 1800, the Jews were two-thirds of the population of Sierpc. The shtetl was a center of industry and commerce, and inhabitants of the surrounding villages visited the town on market days. But the Jewish majority did not last very long. In the year before the start of World War II, Jews accounted for only 30 per cent ofthe population. The wooden synagogue of Sierpc was destroyed by fire and a new synagogue was built in 1895, in the same location.

Avraham Tac, a Holocaust survivor, visited his hometown of Sierpc in 1945, and wrote in Sierpc's Yizkor (Memorial) Book, *"The Jewish Street, starting from the old Beit Midrash, sported a new sidewalk that led over the hills. However, this was not an ordinary sidewalk. Oh, no! Gravestones from our cemetery were used to pave the sidewalk."*

Śniadowo, Poland
Yiddish: Shnodovo

The Jewish settlement in Śniadowo dates from the second half of the 16th century and in 1768, an imposing wooden synagogue was built.

Jewish people engaged in crafts, trading honey, corn, and flax, building products, wood products, and agricultural tools. In 1857, 1,081 Jews, about 89.8% of the population, lived there and by the end of the 19th century the number grew to about 3,000 people.

During World War I, the Russians expelled the Jews from Śniadowo, destroyed the village and set the synagogue on fire. By 1921, only 386 Jews remained in Śniadowo. In the interwar period, anti-Semitism was prevalent. In 1941, after the occupation of the shtetl by the Germans, a group of about fifty Jews were murdered. Another twenty-five Śniadowo Jews hid in the Czerwony Bór forest. When the hideout was discovered in the autumn of 1942, the German military murdered those in the forest during a raid.

Sobkow, Poland
Yiddish: Sobkov

Blessing of the Moon

Sobkow was founded as a city in 1563 by Grand Treasurer of the Crown Stanisław Sobek. The first mention of Jews was in 1662 when there were four Jewish taxpayers. After the third partition of Poland in 1795, Sobkow became part of the Congress of Poland, which was under Russian control.

During the first half of the 19th century Sobkow experienced rapid growth. By 1858, Jews made up 60% of the population. In 1858 the shtetl had a wooden synagogue, rabbi's house, mikvah, cheder, kosher slaughterhouse and a cemetery. The nobleman who owned the shtetl took part in the failed Uprising of 1868. The Russians removed the noblemen and downgraded Sobkow from a town to a village. Fairs could no longer be held, causing the shtetl to decline. Sobkow Jews began to leave for larger towns and America. During World War I much of the town was destroyed by fire.

On August 28, 1942, the Sobków Jews were deported to the ghetto in Jędrzejów and after several days, to the death camp in Treblinka.

Suchowola Poland
Yiddish name: Suchavola

Suchowola, a small shtetl, stood between Bialystok and Grodno. Before World War II the population of Suchowola consisted of 1,000 Christians and 2,000 Jews. The Jews were mostly engaged in commerce and trade. Many were self-employed shoemakers, carpenters, tailors, and saddlers. The Jewish traders supplied grain, fruit and vegetables to Bialystok and Grodno by railway or by horse wagons.

The wooden synagogue of Suchowola dates to the second half of the 18th century. The square men's synagogue was built lower than the entrance room, giving greater height to the synagogue without it appearing higher than the church steeple, which was forbidden. In the shtetl's Yizkor book, "*The Destruction of Suchowola*," Symcha Lazar writes: "*The older generation frequented the synagogues and the houses of study where discussions and everyday quarrels and reconciliations took place; the Jews were attached to their shtetl and were concerned with the well-being of the community. The young people of Suchowola would meet in the library. In short – our Suchowola was a dear little shtetl.*"

The synagogue of Suchowola and the Jewish presence were destroyed by the Germans during World War II.

Warka, Poland
Yiddish: Vorke

The wooden synagogue of Warka was built sometime between 1811-1817. The prayer hall, almost square with an octagonal ceiling, was covered entirely with paintings of animals, symbols, and landscapes. Prayer verses and sayings of the old sages were placed between the images.

During the night after the Jewish holiday of Sukkot in October 1939, the townspeople noticed the synagogue on fire. They ran toward the synagogue to put out the fire. However, the entire Jewish quarter was encircled by soldiers, opening fire at the oncoming Jews, forcing them to retreat to their homes. The fire spread to nearby houses and the Jews attempted to escape, but they were met by bullets. As more Jewish houses caught fire, the people ran to the courtyards for protection against the flames and bullets. Miraculously, the wind changed, and the fire spread to the Christian quarter. When that happened, the soldiers ordered the Jews to work at extinguishing the fire, saving many Jews from certain death.

Wasilkow, Poland
Yiddish: Vashulkova

Wasilków is located seven miles from Bialystok. A Jewish community existed before 1694, when many arrived as refugees from Germany and were given certain privileges in the town. By 1807, the population was 677 inhabitants, with a Jewish majority, whose population increased during the mid-1800's due to the development of the textile and timber industries in the region. The town was inhabited by several groups of peoples with different religions and languages. In 1860 there were 1381 inhabitants, representing various religions: 65 Russian–Orthodox (Belarussians and Russian); 19 Evangelists (Germans); 817 Catholics (Poles and Lithuanians) and 480 Jews. This ethnic diversity played a role in inspiring a native son of Bialystok, Ludwig Zamenhof, to invent Esperanto in hopes of creating an artificial language that could unite the diversity of cultures.

On June 27, 1941, Wasilkow was occupied by German forces. The final liquidation of Wasilkow's Jewish community began on the eve of November 2, 1942, when all Jewish people were transferred to a labor camp where many starved to death within a week or two. The survivors were crammed into cattle cars heading for Treblinka, where they were murdered in gas chambers upon arrival.

Wyszokie Mazowieckie, Poland

Yiddish: Visoka-Mazovietzk

Wysokie Mazowieckie is a small town west of Bialystok. The settlement was first documented in 1239 and received town status in 1502. A Jewish population was first noted in the 17th century. By the second half of the 19th century the Jews had become the majority of the town's citizens.

The beautiful synagogue of Wysokie Mazowieckie was built between the end of the 17th century and the beginning of the 18th century. We know what the synagogue looked like from the research and drawings of Zygmunt Gloger, a Polish historian, archaeologist, geographer, and ethnographer. Over the years, the wooden synagogue deteriorated beyond repair and was dismantled in 1871. A new modern stone synagogue was built to replace it in 1879.

In August 1941 during the German occupation, Wysokie Mazowiecki's Jewish population was sent to a ghetto where they remained until its liquidation on November 2, 1942. From there, the town's remaining two thousand Jews were sent to the Zambrow camp and finally to Auschwitz in January 1943.

Zabłudów, Poland

Yiddish name: Zablodove

The wooden synagogue of Zabłudów was built between 1637-1649 in a town that had a thriving Jewish community for hundreds of years. It had a remarkable three-story roof which was constructed without the use of nails. Renovated and enlarged in 1765, it was considered a Jewish cultural treasure of Poland. Inscribed on its walls were colorful paintings and prayers. There was a large collection of valuable worship vessels of great historical value, including ancient scrolls, a massive silver Torah crown, and a menorah standing on a pole built especially for it. In addition, there were colorful embroidered silk and velvet Torah curtains using silver and gold threads. The beautiful bimah, standing in the middle of the synagogue, was designed in the shape of a tower with windows and arches. A special Sabbath afternoon custom was for the klezmer band, headed by the jester/humorist of the town, coming to play music in the synagogue.

Zabłudów's synagogue and most of the town was burned by German Wehrmacht troops on June 26, 1941. The next year, the ghetto was liquidated, and 1,400 Jews were transported to Treblinka, where all were killed the same day.

BELARUS

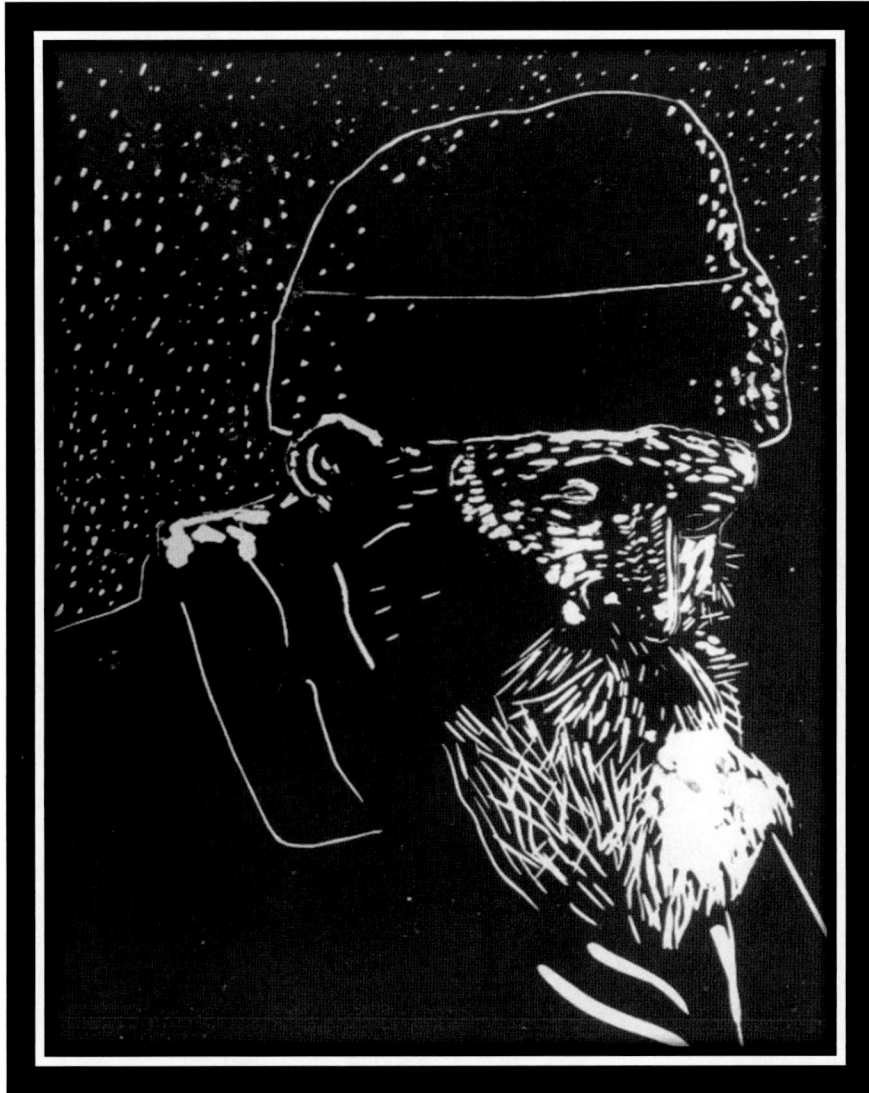

**Byaroza ~ Byeshankovichy ~ Dubroŭna
Hrodna ~ Kazhan-Haradok ~ Lunna
Mahilyow ~ Narowlya ~ Ozëry ~ Pinsk
Sapotskin ~ Uzlyany ~ Vileyka
Vitsyebsk ~ Volpa ~ Zhlodin**

Byaroza, Belarus
Yiddish: Kartoz-Brezah ~ Polish: Bereza Kartuska

The village of Byaroza was first mentioned in 1477. In the 17th century, the village was owned by the Sapieha family, who founded a fortified monastery. The Carthusian order gave its name to the second part of the town's name, Byaroza-Kartuzskaya.

In 1842, a new road was opened between Moscow and Warsaw, passing through the town, which generated a period of economic prosperity. The Jews' sources of income were the "road" and the Yasolda River. Along the road, caravans of merchandise and mail passed and utilized the town's horse-changing stations. This was a source of income for horse traders, horse breeders, and wagon owners. Jews also operated warehouses filled with grain and hay, as well as taverns, restaurants, and inns for travelers.

The Yasolda River was the secondary means of transportation. The area was forested, and in the winter, peasants brought trees they cut down in summer to the riverbanks. With the melting of the snow, they tied the trees into rafts and floated them downriver to Danzig. The wood trade was entirely in the hands of Jews.

The Red Army captured Byaroza in 1939 and made it part of the Belarusian SSR. Following the outbreak of war with the Soviets, the Germans seized the town and occupied it until July 15, 1944, when it was liberated by Red Army troops. During the war, more than 8,000 people were killed in mass executions or starved to death.

Byeshankovichy, Belarus

Yiddish: Byeshankovichy ~ Polish: Bieszankowicze

Linocut based on a woodcut by Solomon Yudovin

Byeshankovichy was a small village in the Grand Duchy of Lithuania. In 1630, the village was purchased by Kazimierz Leon Sapieha. It underwent rapid expansion and was granted the right to hold fairs in 1634. The nobility encouraged Jewish traders to settle in the town. New stone houses were built, and trade fairs were held semi-annually, frequented by 4,000 to 5,000 visitors from Belarus, Russia and abroad.

After the first partition of Poland in 1772, control of the village was passed to the Russian Empire. By 1900, Byeshankovichy was primarily Jewish, numbering 3,182 and representing four fifths of the population. The town had a wooden synagogue, prayer houses, three benevolent societies, and numerous religious schools.

During World War II, Byeshankovichy fell under German control. The entire Jewish population was murdered.

Artist Spotlight: Solomon Yudovin

Byeshankovichy, Belarus
Woodcut by Solomon Yudovin

Solomon Yudovin, Portrait by Bill Farran

A View of Vitebsk -
Woodcut by
Solomon Yudovin

The works of Solomon Yudovin served as an inspiration for many of Bill Farran's linocuts.

Born in the Vitebsk Region of the Russian Empire in the small shtetl of Beshankovichy, Solomon Yudovin became a graphic artist and photographer. He studied first with Yudaha Pen and later with Mstislav Dobujinsky. Both men were teachers of Marc Chagall.

Yudovan's uncle was Shloyme Zanvl Rappoport , known as S Ansky. Between 1911 and the 1914 outbreak of World War I, S. Ansky organized a large-scale ethnographic expedition to study Jewish folklore in the shtetls of Eastern Europe. As a young artist Yudovin joined his uncle as an artist and photographer. His drawings, photographs, and woodcuts have provided us with a picture of shtetl life prior to World War I.

Dubroŭna, Belarus
Yiddish: Dubrovno ~ Polish: Dobrowa

By 1898, there was a significant Jewish community in Dubroŭna, representing more than half the town's population. It was a center for weaving, especially woolen tallits (shawl worn by Jewish men during prayers). Prior to the establishment of a factory in 1750, tallitot were made in small family operations. In the early 1900's there were four factories employing more than six hundred families.

Dubroŭna had been part of the Commonwealth of Poland and Lithuania, later becoming part of Russia in the first partition of Poland (1772) and part of the Soviet Union in 1919. In 1929 the synagogue building was given to the Poland Communist Party to use as a meeting place. The following year Joseph Stalin issued a decree stating that no place of worship should be converted for other use unless a majority of the concerned and the Soviet Central Executive Committee approved. In 1930 the Jews requested that the synagogue be returned to the Jewish Community. When the request was denied, the Jews took over the synagogues and changed the locks.

During World War II the town was occupied by German forces. The town's Jews were killed despite considerable partisan activity. In June 1944 it was liberated by Soviet troops.

Hrodna, Belarus
Yiddish Grodne ~ Polidh: Grodno

The Bialystok district, of which Hrodna became part, experienced a turbulent history. As a border region between Poles, Lithuanians, Russians, and Ukrainians, it was often subject to military attack. Jews played an incredibly significant role in city life as industrialists, merchants, craftsmen, owners of printing houses, doctors, and teachers. It was thought there was a special "Hrodna Aura," that was created by its cultured and intelligent population. Thus, Hrodna was one of the Jewish intellectual capitals of Europe.

The wooden synagogue of Grodno, known as the Zaniomanskaja Synagogue , was built in 1750. It was damaged by fire in 1899 and rebuilt adding two corner buildings It was destroyed by the Nazis during World War II.

According to Nazi records, 44,049 Hrodna Jews from the city and neighboring townlets were sent to the extermination camps. Early in 1942, Jewish underground resistance, defense, and Zionist movements were formed. Approximately 180 Jews remained hidden in the city and district until the town was liberated by the Soviet Army on July 14, 1944. Following its liberation, about 2,000 Jews resettled in Hrodna. In the 1990s the revived community started renovating the stone synagogue built from 1576 to 1580 by Santi Gucci . By early 2000's the synagogue had a resident Chabad rabbi.

Kažhan - Haradok, Belarus
Yiddish: Kozhan-Horodok ~ Polish: Kazhyan-Horadok

Kažhan-Haradok is located on the bank of the Tuna River, near where it comes together with the Prypiat River.

Jews are mentioned in the town from the mid-17th century. The wooden synagogue of Kažhan-Haradok was built in 1780. There were two other synagogues, one belonging to the Stolin Hasidism. Starting with the restrictive May Laws of the 1880's and 1890's the Jews began to leave Kažhan-Haradok. After the pogroms following the Russian defeat in the Russo-Japanese War of 1904-5 and the failed revolution of 1905, emigration increased. Those who had emigrated to America did not forget their old home. As a rule, the remaining Jews of Kažhan-Haradok lived on support from America.

At the beginning of the Holocaust, there were only about eight hundred Jews remaining. The Germans captured the town in 1941. By September 1942 all the Jews of Kažhan-Haradok were murdered and buried in mass graves

41

Lunna, Belarus
Yiddish : Lunna ~ Polish: Lunna

Leon Arkin in his essay, *"I Saw Again My Shtetl Lunna,"* published in the Yiddish newspaper, the "Forward" on June 17, 1949, described the town as follows:

"It would seem that my little shtetl was no different than any of the other little shtetlach that were located in the Jewish area, where Jews were permitted to reside. In our shtetl there were a few rich Jews who were timber merchants and grain merchants. There were also many impoverished Jews. There were also many Talmudic scholars, intellectuals, and ignoramuses. In the market, there were many Jewish shopkeepers who earned their livelihood from the indigenous peasants of the area. The peasants would come to sell their merchandise and at the same time purchase household items and other necessary products. There were also craftsmen who earned a living from their toil. There were individuals who bound wood and individuals who would go around in peasant wagons in order to find some work. There were also poor people, in order to feed their families but did not find work. This was what the people of my shtetl were like."

Mahilyow, Belarus
Yiddish: Molev ~ Polish: Mohylew

The first record of Jews in Belarus was in the 14th century when it was a region within the Poland-Lithuanian Commonwealth and referred to as Belorussia. Despite being under the protection of the Polish crown, the Jews of Mahilyow frequently had problems with their Russian neighbors, resulting in many pogroms.

The wooden synagogue, referred to as the "Cold Synagogue," was built around 1680. It was called the Cold Synagogue because there was no central heating. The interior was almost entirely covered with magnificent colorful folk paintings made in the 1740s by Chaim ben Yitzchak ha-Levi Segal. In the beginning of the 20th century, several ethnographic expeditions, led by Shloyme Zanvl Rappoport, known by his pseudonym S. Ansky (or S. An-sky) and Solomon Yudovin documented and photographed the interiors of the synagogue. The synagogue was closed in 1938 and then dismantled by the Soviet authorities.

Mahilyow was conquered by Wehrmacht forces on 26 July 1941 and remained under German occupation until 28 June 1944. During that period, the Jews of Mogilev were ghettoized and systematically murdered.

Mahilyow Synagogue, Wall Paintings

Narowlya, Belarus
Yiddish: *Narovla* ~ Polish: *Narowla*

Narowlya is in southern Belarus near the Ukranian border on the Pripyat River. There has been a Jewish presence in the town since the 18th century, but little is known about the early history. As a rule, nobility invited Jews to live and work on their estates. There was a large wooden synagogue built inthe middle of the 19th century. In addition, there was a two-story palace, now in ruin, built by the town's owner, David Horvatt, in 1830. From these two artifacts one can recreate Narowlya's history. The large synagogue and palace indicate that the relationship between the nobles and the Jews was profitable for both.

In 1793, Narowlya, along with the rest of Belarus, became part of the Russian Empire known as the Pale of Settlement. According to the census of 1897, more than 1,000 Jews lived here, accounting for 92.5% of the population. After the Russian Revolution, the palace became state owned and badly vandalized. The Soviet Communist government closed the synagogue for worship in 1919. During World War II, as the Nazi army moved into Soviet Russia, many Belorussian Jews attempted to escape but most were unsuccessful. Jews were murdered by both SS troops and by local Belorussian police.

After the disaster at the Chernobyl nuclear power plant in 1986, Narowlya was in part of the contaminated zone of voluntary resettlement. Today its population is about eight thousand people and there are no Jews.

Ozëry, Belarus
Yiddish: Ozra ~ Polish: Jeziory

The wooden synagogue of Ozëry was erected in the mid-1700s. Ozëry was known as a place for Torah study, attracting young men from the surrounding district. The main sources of Jewish livelihood were sawmills, lake fishing, tanning and other crafts.

Zionist activity started at the beginning of the 20th century, and groups supporting the labor parties in Eretz Israel were active before World War II. Ozëry had a center for training Jewish pioneers for the agricultural settlements of Palestine, and many Jews from Ozëry emigrated to Eretz Israel. Jews from the town were among the pioneers of Jewish colonization in Argentina.

The Jewish presence in the town ended on November 11, 1942, when the Jewish population of 1,370 from the Ozëry ghetto were transferred to the Kelbasin forced-labor camp near Grodno and were all deported to death camps a few weeks later.

Pinsk, Belarus
Yiddish: Pinsk ~ Polish: Pinsk

Jews first settled in Pinsk in the 15th century.

During the years after the Partition of Poland (1795), Pinsk developed into an industrial city. Under Russian rule, policies were implemented to decrease the power and wealth of the Polish nobility. As the nobles lost their estates, the Jews lost their special privileges and were economically forced to move to larger towns and cities like Pinsk.

After the assassination of Czar Alexander II in 1881, thousands of shtetls were downgraded from market towns to villages where Jews were forbidden to reside. Thus, many Jews from the area resettled in Pinsk where thousands of Jewish workers found steady employment. By the beginning of World War I, Pinsk was a leading industrial and commercial center.

During World War II, Germany occupied Pinsk in July 1941. Most Jews were killed in late October 1942 during the liquidation of the Pinsk Ghetto by the German Ordnungspolizei and the Belarusian Auxiliary Police, with 10,000 murdered in one day.

Sapotskin, Belarus
Yiddish: Sopotkin ~ Polish: Sopockonie

Sapotskin is a small town in Belarus north-east of Grodno. Situated on the road connecting Grodno and Kovno, the town prospered on trade and forest products.

During World War I, the citizens of Sapotskin suffered at the hands of the Russians and Germans as the town was occupied and liberated several times. Sapotskin became part of Poland in 1921 and suffered under the new anti-Semitic Polish government.

In September 1939 at the beginning of World War II, Sapotskin was occupied by Soviet troops and incorporated into the Byelorussian SSR. In June 1941, the Germans invaded the Soviet Union and set fire to Sapotskin. The Germans ordered the Jews to dig mass graves and bury the dead. When the Germans asked local Poles to identify Jews who collaborated during the Soviet occupation, they obliged, and those Jews were executed. The Sapotskin Ghetto was liquidated in January 1943, when they were sent to Auschwitz where almost all were murdered. Only a few survived the Holocaust, including those protected by the Christian Falejczyk and Bykowski families, later named by Yad Vashem as Righteous Among the Nations.

Uzlyany, Belarus
Yiddish: Ulison ~ Polish: Uzlyany

Uzlyany is a small town in the Minsk region of Belarus. Jews were first mentioned as living there in the second half of the 17ᵗʰ century.

The wooden synagogue was built in the first decade of the18th century. The structure was simple and poor and appropriate for the small and modest congregation. In this humble Prayer House, there was one thing that earned attention, and that was the Torah Ark, the work of wood carver Baer Ben Israel. His father was also a wood carver, and their wonderful creations decorated synagogues in the small towns of that area.

Uzlyany was the birthplace and boyhood home of David Sarnoff, the American businessman and pioneer of American radio and television. Throughout most of his career he led the Radio Corporation of America (RCA) in various capacities from shortly after its founding in 1919 until his retirement in 1970.

In 1923, the Jewish population numbered 541. In June 1941 it was occupied by the Germans who murdered the town's Jews at the Jewish cemetery in October 1941. Uzlyany was liberated by the Red Army in July 1944.

Vileyka, Belarus
Yiddish: Vileyka ~ Polish: Wilejka

Vilyeyka was a small village when it became part of Russia because of the partition of Poland. Tzarina Catherine the Great promoted the village to the status of a district town in the newly formed province of Minsk.

The first settlers in Vilyeyka were mostly Jews who lived in nearby villages and farms. Vilyeyka experience rapid growth in the 1880's as Jews were expelled from rural villages and forced to relocate to towns. Another step in the advancement of Vilyeyka was the establishment of a railway station in the town along the new Shedletz- Bologoe line built in 1904. This was a big stride towards further development.

In 1860 there were three synagogues in Vilyeyka: the great Wooden Synagogue, the Beit Midrash of the Koidanow Hasidim, and the "Shtiebel" (small, informal house of prayer) of the Lubavitch Hasidim. During World War I most houses and synagogues in the town were destroyed by fire. Most of the inhabitants left the town for fear of the Cossacks.

Vilyeyka was always a town of Zionist activity and as soon as World War I ended, Jewish youth renewed the activities that were forbidden during the years of the war. They flocked to the various Zionist organizations and groups. Many young were trained and prepared for Aliya to Eretz Israel.

During World War II, the Nazis destroyed all Jewish life in Vilyeyka.

Vitsyebsk, Belarus
Yiddish: Vitebsk ~ Polish: Witevsk

Linocut Fashioned After a Woodcut by Solomon Yudovin

Vitsyebsk is one of the oldest European settlements and had a long Jewish presence. The first synagogue was built in 1627.

In modern times, Vitsyebsk was a large modern city with trade, industry, and culture. One hundred years ago, there were twenty-seven churches, and over fifty synagogues and prayer houses that included a large Hasidic presence.

There was an art school in Vitsyebsk, run by Yehuda M. Pen, which trained many leading artists including Marc Chagall and Solomon Yudovin. It is from their artwork that we can see the wooden synagogues of Vitsyebsk.

Because of the fighting during World War II, the Holocaust, and post war Soviet rule, all the synagogues, both wooden and stone, were destroyed. There are a handful of photos left to document the rich Jewish life of Vitsyebsk. World War II was very destructive for the people of Vitsyebsk. Almost all its Jews were murdered and very few Christians survived the fighting between the Nazis and the Red Army.

Volpa, Belarus
Yiddish: Volp ~ Polish: Wolpa

According to legend a Polish nobleman and his son were travelling through the area when the son became very ill. The Jews of Volpa nursed the boy back to health. To show his appreciation, the nobleman had a synagogue built in 1643. It is considered one of the most significant synagogues in Poland, containing a beautiful carved raised bimah with four supporting pillars.

Because there was no stove for heat, it was used daily during the summer but open only on Saturdays during winter. The people would tell the Rabbi, "*Make it fast—it's cold!*"

Besides their traditional occupations in commerce and crafts, the Jews of Volpa engaged in domestic farming. Lack of rail connections prevented further industrial development, so they became expert gardeners and tobacco growers. Following World War I, and the beginning of Polish rule in 1919, the armies stationed near Volpa incited anti-Jewish activity. In 1929, when Jews were forbidden to grow tobacco, their main source of livelihood, some became vegetable farmers, specializing in cucumbers and pickling.

The wooden synagogue was burned down by the Nazis in November 1942. It is believed that only one Jewish resident who lived in Volpa prior to the German invasion survived the war.

Zhlodin, Belarus
Yiddish: Zhlodin ~ Polish: Zlobin

Zhlodin was first mentioned in the 15th century. Sadly, the first mention of the Jewish community, referred to a pogrom against the Zhlodin Jews in 1768. The pogrom was staged by the Ukrainian paramilitary Hidamaks whose goals were the destruction of the Polish Catholic Nobles and the removal of the Jews.

In 1793, the settlement became part of the Russian Empire. This contributed to the growth of the Jewish population. In 1873 the Libau-Romny railway passed through Zhlodin and boosted the town's growth. The railroad connected Romny Ukraine with the ice-free port in Libau, on the Baltic Sea in present-day Latvia. By the 1880s, the Jewish population of Zhlobin reached its peak. Jews owned over 50% of the houses in the city, comprising 82.2% of the total population. and had five synagogues in the city in which to worship.

By the time Zhlobin was captured by the Nazis in August 1941, many Jews had a chance to evacuate. Those who were left behind were forced into two tiny ghettos. The Jewish community of Zhlobin was destroyed in April 1942

LITHUANIA

Bimah

Jurbarkas ~ Kelme ~ Prienai

Šaukėnai ~ Šiaulėnai ~ Valkininkai

Vilkovishk

Jurbarkas, Lithuania
Yiddish: Yurburg ~ Polish: Jurbork

Jurbarkas is first mentioned in a Jewish context in the 1590's. In 1766, the Jewish population was 2,333. The community maintained a cemetery and a few prayer houses, among them the magnificent wooden synagogue built in 1790, one of the oldest in Lithuania. The synagogue was world famous for the wooden carved Aron Kodesh (Holy Ark). People found it hard to believe how such wonderful birds, animals and flowers could be carved out of wood, climbing from the floor all the way up to the ceiling.

The community was strongly influenced by the Haskalah ideas, a modernizing Jewish movement. In 1884, the local Talmud Torah began to teach mathematics and Russian in addition to traditional subjects.

After the German invasion in June 1941, mass shootings began. The Jews were forced to tear down the old wooden synagogue. Three days later Torah scrolls and religious books were burned. Murders continued until September. On October 1, the mayor reported that no Jews remained in Jurbarkas. However, a few individuals survived, some joining the partisans.

Kelmė, Lithuania
Yiddish: Kelm ~ Polish: Kelmy

The wooden synagogue of Kelmė stood for approximately three hundred years. According to legend, the town was owned by Poritz (noble landowner) Grozheviski, who lived on a large estate outside the town. The Poritz had no male heir, and in desperation for a son, he asked the Jews to pray for him. To show his gratitude for their prayers when his wife gave birth to a son later that year, the Poritz built a synagogue for the town's Jews and freed them from taxes.

While the synagogue may not have been the largest, it was famous for its ancient artifacts throughout Lithuania. Built of wood with a wooden shingle roof reminiscent of a pagoda, its style was common in Eastern Europe.

According to the 1923 census there were 1,599 Jews living in Kelmė. Most were small shopkeepers and artisans, but there were also grain and timber merchants as well as owners of brush factories and tanneries.

The Germans occupied Kelmė shortly after the outbreak of war between Germany and the Soviet Union during World War II. The shtetl's Jews were murdered between July and August 1941.

Prienai, Lithuania
Yiddish: Pren ~ Polish: Preny

Fiddle player based on Martina Shapiro's "Shtetl Fiddler"

Prienai is in the southern part of Lithuania on the shores of the Neman River. The town was built on both sides of the river, the main part being on the left side of the river, with a bridge linking both parts.

Prienai was first mentioned in 1502. Until 1795, Prienai was part of the Polish-Lithuanian Commonwealth. The third division of Poland split the town into a Prussian portion and a Russian portion using the river as the new border. Smuggling became a new and major industry. In 1868 a beer brewery, Goldberg's Brewery, was established there and became famous throughout Lithuania because of the quality of its products.

In April 1915, during World War I, the German army was advancing into Russia. Fearing that the Jews would be favor the Germans, the Russian military authorities expelled Jews from the town forcing them deeper into Russia away from the front. When the German army occupied Prienai, many Jews returned home, finding their houses, their synagogues, ritual baths, and the cemetery ruined and robbed by the retreating Russians,

The Prienai synagogue was destroyed during World War II.

Šaukėnai, Lithuania
Yiddish: Shukian ~ Polish: Szawkiany

The wooden synagogue of Šaukėnai, built in the eighteenth century, was famous for its beautiful carved bimah and Aron Kodesh.

On August 29th, 1941, the Jews of Šaukėnai were taken to the town of Zhager where many Jews from the nearby towns had already been confined. All were murdered on October 2,1941.

Eight youngsters, who had managed to escape from the Zhager massacre, sought asylum with the priest of Šaukėnai. He proposed that they become Christians, to which they agreed, but this did not rescue them. They too were shot and buried in the Catholic cemetery where a cross marks their grave. Early in the 1990's a tablet was erected on their graves, with the following inscription:

"Here eight Jewish youngsters are buried. They were murdered on November 1, 1941, All Saints Day. All were led to the ghetto of Zhager, but survived by escaping from there, after which they found asylum in the church of Šaukėnai. At the end of September 1941, they received the Holy Cross. Priest Jonas Stasevicius baptized and adopted them, but this was not enough for the murderers and their leaders. These youngsters died because they were born Jews. Rest in peace."

Šiaulėnai, Lithuania
Yiddish: Shavlan ~ Polish: Szawlany

Siauliai was established as early as the 13th century, and the first Jews settled in the city four hundred years later, during the 17th century. Some of them arrived as refugees from the pogroms conducted by Bogdan Khmelnytsky against Ukrainian and Polish Jews during the Khmelnitsky Uprising (1648 - 1649).

During World War I, the Siaulenai Jews were exiled to regions in the Russian interior. After the proclamation of Lithuanian independence (1918), many of the Jews returned to the town. Due to the economic situation, the town's Jews began to grow vegetables and fruits. Many Jewish families in the town were forced to rely on assistance from relatives who had emigrated to the United States and South Africa. The number of Jews in the town fell annually due to emigration to larger cities and abroad.

When the German army conquered Lithuania in June 1941, only twenty Jewish families lived in Siaulenai. In September 1941, they were transferred to Zhager and massacred together with the local Jews.

Valkininkai, Lithuania
Yiddish: Olkenik ~ Polish: Olkieniki

The Valkininkai synagogue was built at the end of the wooden synagogues period. A worshipers' meeting took place in 1790 and they demanded that a new synagogue be built after the old synagogue burned down. The construction started in 1798 and was completed two years later. The outside looked like a Chinese pagoda–a typical synagogue style of that period.

The Ark was covered with a *parochet*, the curtain over the Aron Kodesh (Torah Ark). The parochet in Valkininkai was incredibly famous. It is told that when Napoleon Bonaparte passed through the town on his way to Russia, he admired the artwork of the synagogue's interior. In appreciation, he ordered a section cut from the cover under his saddle and gave it to the town and to the synagogue. The town's leaders prepared a parochet from the cover. The words "Gloria et Patria" (for glory and fatherland) were embroidered on the parochet's corners.

During the first days of the Lithuanian occupation by Nazi Germany, all the town's synagogues were burned down.

Vilkovishk, Lithuania
Yiddish: Vilkovishk ~ Polish: Wylkowyszki

It is believed that the first Jews arrived in Vilkaviškis in the fourteenth century.

At the beginning of the sixteenth century Queen Bona, the wife of King Zigmunt August II, donated timber to the citizens of Vilkaviškis for building prayer houses. Jews were among the beneficiaries, and they built their synagogue in 1545, which existed until World War II. It contained a grandiose oak Aron Kodesh (Holy Ark), three stories high, decorated with artistically engraved wooden ornaments, housing the Sefer Torah (Five Books of Moses) and several scrolls brought by those expelled from Spain.

Shortly after the outbreak of World War II, the Soviets gained control of Vilkaviškis. On June 22, 1941, the Nazi German army, with assistance from Lithuanian collaborators, occupied the town. Many Jewish homes and the synagogue were destroyed by bombing. A few weeks later the Jews were imprisoned in a ghetto set up in military barracks outside of town. Many Jewish men were shot and murdered on July 28, 1941, and buried in two pits, which were prepared in advance. On September 24, the Jewish women and children were shot at the same location. According to Soviet sources, a total of 3,056 people were murdered at that time.

UKRAINE

Synagogue Western Wall Entrance

**Berezdivtsi~ Dolyna ~ Horodok ~ Horokhiv
Hvizdets ~ Kamyanka-Buzka ~ Khodoriv
Kitajgorod ~ Mychajliwka ~ Myn'kivtsi
Novyy Yarychiv ~ Olyka ~ Pavlivka
Pechenizhyn ~ Pogrebishche~ Skelivka ~Smotrich
Tal'ne ~ Yabluniv ~ Yarmolyntsi ~ Zarechanka
Zhydachiv ~ Zolochiv**

Berezdivtsi, Ukraine
Yiddish: Brizdivitz ~ Polish: Brzozowce

The Jewish community of Berezdivtsi dates to the late 17th century. By the late 19th century there were around five hundred Jews and in 1921, the Jewish population numbered four hundred and forty.

Berezdivtsi's Jewish community had a large wooden synagogue. In front of the prayer room for the men, there was a vestibule and next to it another room for the kehillah (the elected self-governing body). Above was the women's prayer room, which only allowed a view into the main room through narrow slits. Access to the women's room was via a staircase along the south wall.

The three outer sides of the men's prayer room each had two pairs of windows. The bimah was not placed in the middle of the room but was offset towards the entrance. The walls and ceiling were covered by colorful folk paintings, which had faded by the beginning of the 20th century. The only paintings of figures and signs of the zodiac in the vaulted ceiling were still visible.

The town was occupied by Germans in June 1941. On September 5, 1942, the Jews of Berezdivtsi were deported to the Belzec extermination camp.

Dolyna, Ukraine
Yiddish: Yanov ~ Polish: Janów

Image of Jewish Wedding based on Zamy Steynowitz' "Jewish Wedding" SE514 with permission. All Rights to the original reserved to the Steynowitz Estate.

The city's history began in the 10th century, making it one of the oldest in the region.

The first Jewish families started to settle in Dolyna in the 16th century. The profitable salt trade attracted new settlers to the town and resulted in the rapid growth of the Jewish community. In the first Partition of Poland, Dolyna became part of the Austro-Hungarian Empire. By the end of the 19th century big fires had destroyed the town completely. The first decade of the new century was devoted to the revival of the town.

During World War II the city was occupied first by the Soviet Union (September 1939 - June 1941), then by Hungary (July 1941), and finally by Germany (August 1941- 1944). During the German occupation, the Jewish population was murdered.

Dolyna Interior, Steps to the Bimah

Horodok, Ukraine
Yiddish: Grayding ~ Polish: Gródek

Horodok was first mentioned in historical documents in the year 1392. Jews were invited to settle in Horodok by the noble family who owned the town during the 1500's. The Jewish community grew and prospered in the late 1640's and early 1650's.

During the Khmelnitsky massacres the town was devastated and the Jewish community was gravely affected by Cossack raids. In 1653 Bogdan Khmelnitsky's army of 30,000 men besieged the town. Poles, Ukrainian Uniates (a church adhering to Eastern rites but submitting to Papal authority) and Jews hid behind the walls of Horodok Castle. Cossacks took the castle by storm, destroyed it, and massacred everybody. As recorded by one of Bogdan Khmelnitsky contemporaries, "*... they spared neither nobility nor riffraff.*" After the Khmelnitsky Rebellion the Jews recovered and were once again prosperous.

The great wooden synagogue was built during a period of peace and prosperity. Until the Partition of Poland, Horodok was part of the Polish-Lithuanian Commonwealth. After the Partition of Poland, Horodok was located within the Russian Empire. After World War I Horodok became part of Poland. At the end of World War II, the town was Ukrainian. The Jewish presence in Horodok was ended by the Nazis in World War II.

Horokhiv, Ukraine
Yiddish: Horochov ~ Polish: Horochów

Horokhiv was first mentioned in 1450 when King Kazimierz Jagielonczyk granted Count Olizarov-Szylowicz the fiefdom of Horokhiv as a reward for his services to the crown. Jews first settled in Horokhiv in the 16th Century. Their large wooden Great Synagogue was a high building, covered with a tin roof, and crowned by a dome.

In 1791 Count Stanislav Poniatowski acquired Horokhiv and developed the growth of trade by introducing weekly market days important to Jewish commerce. Between the end of World War I until the Holocaust, Jews numbered about five thousand people of the town's eight thousand. In the years 1933-34, the Polish government took measures designed to force Jews from their favorable economic position. When a large Polish department store opened in Horokhiv, it struck a severe blow to the livelihood of many Jews.

On June 26, 1942, the town was seized by German forces, followed by the murder of about three hundred Jews in the municipal park. In September, a ghetto was established with a population of about five thousand people, including two thousand deportees from surrounding areas. On September 8, 1942, the ghetto was liquidated as the Jews were driven out of town and shot at pits previously prepared by German forces. All Jewish life in Horokhiv ended with the Holocaust.

Hvizdets, Ukraine
Yiddish: Gvozdetz ~ Polish: Gwoździec

The history of Hvizdets can be traced to 1557 when a private town was established there, drawing significant income from organizing fairs and markets. By 1635 there was a Jewish presence. Their wooden synagogue was built between 1640-1650. When the synagogue was reconfigured during 1700-1730, it was built in the Baroque style, the first of its kind in the area. Hebrew inscriptions and colorful animal figures covered the ceiling and walls. The synagogue's cupola was replicated three quarter size for the Museum of Polish Jewish History in Warsaw, Poland, as an example of beautiful architecture and design combining religious images and texts, using Jewish and Polish traditions. It was burned down during World War I.

On June 2, 1941, the town was seized by Hungarian troops allied with Germany and replaced by Germans in November. A ghetto was established in early 1942 with 1,540 people. On April 12 Germans and Ukrainians surrounded the ghetto. Jews rushed out as buildings were set on fire, to force those who were still in hiding out. Several hundred Jews were driven to a nearby forest and shot; the town's survivors were forced to collect the bodies and incinerate them. The ghetto was liquidated on September 8, 1942, and the town's Jews were transported to the death camp in Belzec three days later.

Main exhibition of the Museum of the History of Polish Jews in Warsaw.
Reconstruction of the synagogue of Gwoździec, Ukraine
Courtesy of the Museum of the History of Polish Jews

Kamyanka Buzka, Ukraine
Yiddish: Kaminka ~ Polish: Strumiłowa

The presence of Jews in Kamyanka Buzka was first recorded in 1465. In 1589 the Jewish community was permitted to purchase houses, engage in trade, and build a synagogue. The wooden synagogue of Kamyanka Buzka, built in 1627, was exceptionally large and beautiful with a dome over the entrance. It had a main prayer hall, a western two storied annex and gallery under the same roof. The women's section was upstairs with inside staircases.

Kamyanka Buzka was under Soviet control between 1939 and 1941. The Jewish community changed during this time, when community institutions were dissolved, and independent political activity was forbidden. The traditional Jewish economy was also hurt. Jews tried to integrate into new activities by organizing themselves into craftsmen's cooperatives and entering the municipal and civil service.

On June 28, 1941, German Wehrmacht troops occupied the town, and the next day they murdered two hundred Jews. On July 2, the Ukrainians, instigated by the Germans, carried out a pogrom, killing a few hundred Jews. On September 14, 1942, approximately 1500 Jews were deported to the Belzec death camp. The last Jews still living in Kamyanka Buzka were murdered by the Nazis and buried in a mass grave.

Kamyanka Buzka, Holy Ark

Ukrainian Jew

Khodoriv, Ukraine
Yiddish: Khodorov ~ Polish: Chederev

The wooden synagogue of Khodoriv was built in 1652. The exterior was plain and humble, but inside it was decorated with beautiful paintings and elaborate religious articles. The glory of this synagogue was in no small measure due to an itinerant Jewish artist named Israel ben Mordechai Lissnicki, who painted two other synagogues in the area. Although the synagogue of Khodoriv was destroyed during World War II, a model of the ceiling depicting magnificently colored Zodiac signs and Biblical passages can be seen in the ANU Museum in Tel Aviv, Israel.

In July 1941, when German troops occupied Khodoriv, there were about 2,500 Jews. Together with their Ukrainian collaborators, the Germans robbed and abused Jews and burned down the Great Synagogue. During the first Aktion in June 1942, 1000- 1500 Jews were rounded up. Those too sick or weak were shot; others were sent to Belzec where they were immediately killed. In October, another 350 Jews were deported to Belzec to be murdered. In February 1943, Ukrainian police murdered all but fifteen of the remaining population who had been hidden by friends and acquaintances.

Replica of Wooden Synagogue of Khodoriv, Zodiac
Photo by Bill Farran at ANU Museum
Tel Aviv, Israel. August 2023

Interior of Khodoriv Synagogue

Kitajgorod, Ukraine
Yiddish: Kitaigorod ~ Polish: Kitajgoród

Kitajgorod was founded in 1607 as a fortified town by Andrzej Potocki. His son, Stanisław Potocki, completed the construction of the Kitajgorod Castle in 1638.

During The Russian Civil War, there was a violent pogrom in Kitajgorod on June 16, 1919, when about 80 Jews perished. During the night, a medical team was dispatched to Kitajgorod who set up a makeshift infirmary to provide relief and medical treatment for victims. It also collected information about the events preceding and during the pogrom and recorded the numbers of casualties.

The team inspected the homes in the shtetl to assess the extent of damage, injuries, and loss of life. They noted the shattered glass in the windows and the broken doors of the buildings, which had been emptied of everything including samovars (urns with a faucet at the base used to boil water for tea) making it impossible to boil water to tend to the wounded. *"Traces of bullets are seen on the walls and ceilings of many homes. But most importantly,"* wrote one of the medical team's members, *"there is blood everywhere…Kitaihorod is covered in blood."*

The Germans occupied the town in 1941, sending Jews to a labor camp in Kamenets-Podolski. In January 1942 they were murdered along with other Jews from the area.

Mychajliwka, Ukraine
Yiddish: Mikhalpol ~ Polish: Mikhalpol

Mychajliwka was a small settlement in the Podolsky region of Ukraine. The town was allowed to hold three fairs a year and a weekly bazaar.

An oak wooden synagogue was built in approximately 1760. The entire inner surface of the synagogue was covered with paintings by an artist who signed his name, Yehuda. By the 1930's the synagogue was in such disrepair that it was no longer in use.

The Nazis destroyed the synagogue and the Jewish community in the autumn of 1942.

Myn'kivtsi, Ukraine
Yiddish: Minkovitz ~ Polish: Mińkowce

Jews settled in Myn'kivtsi in the early 18th century and set up trades including a town brewery and two mills. The Jewish community established the institutions required for their autonomous governance: the kahal (governing council), a rabbi, a cantor, and numerous kosher butchers.

By 1788, the community built a large wooden synagogue on the bank of the Ushitsa River. Myn'kivtsi became the possession of Polish noble Ignacy Ścibor Marchocki (1755–1827) . One of Marchocki's first reform acts was to abolish serfdom on his estate and give all people equal rights. It was not until 1861 that Alexander II freed the serfs in the Russian Empire. In 1792, the first Jewish printing houses were opened. The printing industry and Marchocki's reforms continued until his death in 1827. In 1836 the town, no longer owned by a Polish noble, was ruled by the Russian Government.

On July 31, 1941, the German Wehrmacht occupied Myn'kivtsi. The town's Jews were shot and buried in a mass grave on August 30, 1941.

Novyy Yarychiv, Ukraine
Yiddish: Yartchev ~ Polish: Jaryczów Nowy

Jews first settled in Novyy Yarychiv in the 16th century. In 1578, most of the twenty-five Jews of the town were killed during Tatar raids. By 1881 the Jewish population was 1,165.

Every Wednesday was market day, and several times a year there were large fairs. Ukrainian and Polish farmers came to town to buy goods: leather, metal pots, axes, buckets, plows, nails, materials for shirts, dresses, and ribbons. The farmers sold cows, bulls, horses, chickens, wood, many kinds of grain, vegetables, potatoes, and various fruits. At the markets and fairs, Jews bought, sold, and earned their livelihood. Late in the day, especially on summer days when the farmers left town and the dust from their carriages settled, one could see Jews with long black beards and side curls, dressed in long caftans or overcoats and large black velvet hats, rushing to the synagogue, study center, or small places of worship.

In 1941, Nazis occupied the town and established a ghetto in November 1942 for more than 2,500 Novyy Yarychiv Jews and others from surrounding areas. The ghetto was liquidated on January 15th, 1943. One thousand were killed at the Jewish cemetery and another in the nearby forest where a monument was erected at the place of the shooting in 1991.

Olyka, Ukraine
The Legend of Olyka's Synagogue

The Count of the shtetl Olyka was a wicked man. He mistreated both Ukrainian peasants and Jews. One day the Count became seriously ill and sent for the priest, asking him to pray to God for a cure. He promised the priest that if he recovered, he would build a church. However, the Count's health did not improve. In desperation, he asked the town's rabbi to pray for his recovery, and promised if the rabbi's prayers were answered, he would build a synagogue.

Soon after the rabbi prayed for the Count, he was totally cured. He arranged to have a church and a synagogue constructed. Not to anger the Jews or Christians, the Count ordered the two buildings to be built simultaneously. After both buildings were completed, they looked almost identical. When the count came to inspect the buildings, he could not take his eyes off them because of their beauty. The Count became very troubled. The next day he called for the architect and had him put to death, because he could not bear the thought of this architect being invited by another nobleman anywhere else to build something as wonderful.

Olyka, Ukraine
Yiddish: Olik ~ Polish: Olyks

Olyka was settled in the early Middle Ages. During the Protestant Reformation, the town became one of the most important centers of Calvinism in the Polish–Lithuanian Commonwealth. Its growth was halted by the Khmelnitsky Uprising of 1648-1657, during which the town was captured by Cossacks, plundered and burned down, Twenty out of thirty Jewish families survived. During a Cossack raid in 1651. the Jewish and Christian villagers took refuge in the fortified Rodziwill Castle. It was believed that the prayer by Rabbi David Ha Levy Segal miraculously saved them from a certain death.

***Town square with wooden synagogue on the
left and stone synagogue in background***
Photo from S. Ansky Ethnography Expositions 1912-1914

As a result of the Third Partition of Poland in 1795, Olyka was annexed by the Russian Empire. It played an important role as a center of the wood and grain trade in the 19th Century. During World War I, the Jews of Olyka suffered from the fierce battles between the Russian and Austro-Hungarian armies, and pogroms supported by both. The Russian Civil War (1918-1920) once again caused Olyka's Jews to suffer several pogroms committed by the Polish Army, the White Russian Army, and Ukrainian Nationalists. At the end of World War I, Olyka became part of Poland.

Olyka's large Jewish community was destroyed during the Holocaust. After World War II the area was annexed by the Soviet Union and incorporated into the Ukrainian SSR. Since 1991 Olyka has been part of independent Ukraine.

Pavlivka, Ukraine
Yiddish: Poritsk ~ Polish: Porit

Pavlivka, in the Volhynia region of western Ukraine, had been part of the Polish-Lithuanian Commonwealth , later annexed into the Russian Empire after the partition of Poland. After World War I, Pavlivka again became part of Poland. Pavlivka's population was almost 2,000 people, half of whom were Jewish. The Polish and Ukrainian peasants lived in the countryside. All three ethnic groups lived together peacefully until World War II.

In June of 1941, the Nazis captured the region. The Jews of Pavlivka and those of the Volhynia region, numbering about 3,000, were sent into a ghetto. With the help of the Ukrainian police, nine hundred were murdered in a mass execution in September 1942. Once the Jews were gone Ukrainians attempted to force the Polish people out of the region. On July 11, 1943, units of the Ukrainian Insurgent Army murdered Polish inhabitants of the town. Most people were killed during a ceremony in a local Roman Catholic church. Ukrainians entered the church, throwing grenades and finally shooting at them with machine guns and setting fire to the church. The Germans did nothing to prevent this ethnic violence.

Pechenizhyn, Ukraine
Yiddish: Petchinizhin ~ Polish: Petchinizhin

Pechenezhin is a small town in the Carpathian Mountains of western Ukraine on the Luchka and Pecheniga rivers, near Kolomyja. The town was owned by the Potocki family, the biggest Polish landowners in Ukraine.

It is believed Jews resided there as early as the 18th century, since the wooden synagogue in the town, complete with its spectacular wall paintings, dates to this time. The population of the town – both Jewish and non-Jewish – grew significantly following the discovery of oil at the end of the 19th century. In 1890 there were 2,224 Jews in Pechenizhyn of 6,838 inhabitants, but with the decrease in oil production the Jewish population of the town dwindled as citizens left for other locations in Galicia or abroad.

During the Holocaust, the Jews of Pechenizhyn were deported to the Kolomyja ghetto, where they died together with the Jews of Kolomyja.

Prayers Painted on a Pechenezhin Synagogue Wall

Pogrebishche, Ukraine
Yiddish: Probishta ~ Polish: Probisha

Pogrebishche was established in the 12th century. In 1690, the Jews of this small shtetl constructed a wooden synagogue on the ruins of the previous synagogue which had been severely damaged during the Khmelnitsky uprising of 1648-1649, which was a Cossack and peasant uprising against Polish rule in Ukraine, resulting in the destruction of hundreds of Jewish communities.

Following the partition of Poland, Pogrebishche became part of Galicia, Austro-Hungary, populated by Poles, Ukrainians, and Jews. The Jews of Pogrebistche were well known for their self-defense forces during the Russian Civil War of 1918-1920. Almost all Jews were armed with rifles, revolvers, hand grenades, bombs, and more. It was not an uncommon thing to see in the street an old Jew with a long grey beard carrying a rifle on his shoulder. The men of the self-defense detachment were organized on a military basis, holding off many attacks. However, they were disarmed by "friendly government forces" promising to protect them, but who quickly killed them in horrible pogroms.

When the Russians took over Pogrebistche in 1919, the wooden synagogue ceased to be a house of worship. The city was overrun by the Germans on July 21, 1941. On October 18th, over 1,750 Jews were murdered in a nearby forest and the Jewish town of Probishta ceased to exist.

Skelivka, Ukraine
Yiddish: *Felshtin* ~ Polish: *Felsztyn*

The village of Skelivka is located a few miles from the border with Poland and Ukraine in the eastern part of the Carpathian Mountains.

Felsztyn, as the settlement is called in Polish, was founded in 1374 by King Ludwik Węgierski, and received town privileges under the Magdeburg rights in the 1380's. After the first Partition of Poland in 1772 until 1918, the town belonged to the Austro-Hungarian Empire. During the Russian Civil War in 1918, about six hundred Felshtin Jews were murdered during a Cossack pogrom. Between 1918 and 1939 Felsztyn became part of The Second Republic of Poland.

On September 17, 1939, Felsztyn was occupied by the Soviet Union, and renamed Skelevka. On Yom Kippur, 1941, the Nazis forced the Jews of Felshtin into a forest where they were forced to dig a large mass grave in which they were buried alive. After the war, the surviving Jews erected a memorial tombstone above the mass grave.

After the collapse of the Soviet Union in 1991, the town became part of Ukraine and is now Skelivka

In the Midrash

Interior, Skelivka Wooden Synagogue

Smotrich, Ukraine
Yiddish name: Smotritch ~ Polish: Smotrycz

By the beginning of the 18th century there was a Jewish community in Smotrich. A large synagogue, noted for its beauty, was built there in the 18th century. The town was part of the Polish-Lithuanian Commonwealth until 1795 when it was incorporated into the Russian Empire.

When Smotrich became part of the Soviet Union after World War I, all Jewish schools were closed, and teaching in Hebrew was prohibited. However, local Jews kept studying with Torah tutors illegally until the middle of the 1920s. In 1925, a cell of "Hashomer-Hatzair" (Socialist-Zionist, secular Jewish youth movement) of about sixty people was established in Smotrich, which maintained a clandestine connection with its central branch in Kamenets-Podolsky. By the end of 1927, five people were arrested in the town, with the majority being leaders of "Hashomer-Hatsair" and 33 Jewish pupils were expelled from school "for being members of the Zionist organization".

Smotrich was occupied by German troops on July 9th, 1941, and was liberated by the Soviet troops on March 27th, 1944. During the Holocaust 670 Smotrich Jews were murdered.

Tal'ne, Ukraine
Yiddish: Talna ~ Polish: Talnoe

The Jews of Tal'ne were mentioned for the first time in connection with Cossack pogroms when the local Jewish community was destroyed in 1768. In 1848, according to the census, the Jewish community of Tal'ne consisted of 1,807 people, while in 1897, the Jewish population increased to 5,452 people (57%). In 1854, Rabbi David Tversky (1808—1882) arrived in the town, and the place became a center for Hasidim.

A Talmud Torah was opened in 1889, and 59 people studied there at the expense of the community. In 1910, in addition to the Talmud Torah, there was a private Jewish college for men, a synagogue and four other prayer houses. In 1912, the number of pupils had reached about one hundred.

The local Jewish population suffered heavily during the Russian Civil War. There were several pogroms from peasant gangs, as well as the White Army soldiers, who pillaged and burned most of the town in the summer of 1919.

Yabluniv, Ukraine
Yiddish: Yablanov ~ Polish: Jabłonów

Yabluniv is a small town on the Luchka River in the Carpathian Mountains whose local population was heavily Jewish and included Hutsuls, Ukrainians and Hungarians.

During the 19th Century the Jewish community of Yabluniv grew, reaching its highest number during the 1890's. From that point it began to dwindle because of migration to larger cities and overseas countries. This process intensified during World War I because of injuries inflicted on the Jews during intense fighting between Austria-Hungry and Russia. After World War I, Yabluniv, became part of Poland. In the years between World War I and World War II, life became difficult for Yubluniv Jews as Polish boycotts of Jewish businesses made earning a living difficult.

During the first day of Passover 5702 (April 8, 1942), the Gestapo together with the Ukrainian police began the destruction of the Jews of Yabluniv.

Yarmolyntsi, Ukraine
Yiddish: Yarmolintza ~ Polish: Yarmolintza

The earliest known Jewish community in Yarmolyntsi was during the 16th century. However, the town was heavily damaged during the Khmelnitsky pogroms of 1648-49. In 1926, according to the census, the Jewish population was 2700. The wooden synagogue ceased to function as a place of worship when the town became part of the Soviet Union post World War I and religious observance was not permitted.

World War II was disastrous for the Jewish population of Yarmolyntsi after the Nazis occupied the town on July 8, 1941. The next day, 16 Jewish men were shot to death and thrown into a mass grave. Eventually the town's Jews were forced into a ghetto. In October 1942, a mass murder occurred when the Jews from Yarmolyntsi and the surrounding towns were shot to death at the site of a former military base near Yarmolintsi. A group of Jews put up armed resistance and killed a few German soldiers and Ukrainian auxiliary police. The town was liberated by the Red Army on March 27, 1944.

Zarechanka, Ukraine
Yiddish Name: Lantzekronia ~ Polish Name: Lanckoruń

The first reference to Lyantskorun was in the first half of the 16th century. The town was named for the Lyantskoronski family, who owned the village.

The Jewish community was almost eliminated during the Bogdan Khmelnitsky uprising. In the second part of the 18th century the residents of Liantskorun managed to acquire the right to hold fairs in the town. This caused a quick development in trade and attracted new Jewish residents as well.

Zarichanka was captured by the Germans on the ninth of July 1941. There is some information that the local population tried to help the Jews but there is nothing to substantiate this. In the summer of 1942, all the Jews were moved to the ghetto in Kamenets-Podolskiy and were killed together with the local ones.

During the town's liberation from the Nazis by the Soviet Army, it was renamed Zarechanka. A postcard from the synagogue was incorrectly attributed to the Polish town of Lanckorona. The Yiddish name, Lantzekronia, and the Polish name for the town, Lanckoruń, are so like Lanckorona, the name of a southern Polish town, that it is easy to see how an error could have been made.

Zhydachiv, Ukraine
Yiddish: Zhidetshoyv ~ Polish: Zhidetshoyv

Jews lived in Zhydachiv before the middle of the 15th century. The wooden synagogue in Zhydachiv was built in 1727. The Jews of Zhydachiv made their livelihood primarily through trade, diverse types of leasing and the production and sale of alcoholic beverages.

The Jewish community of Zhydachiv is known primarily due to the prominent Hasidic leader Rabbi Tzvi Hirsh Eichenstein, the Rebbe of Zhydachiv, who was active in eastern Galicia during the 19th century. Rabbi Tzvi Hirsh was a prominent figure in the battle against Jewish Enlightenment.

In 1942 many of the Jews of Zhydachiv were murdered by the Nazis and were buried in a mass grave. In September 1942, the town the Jews called Zhidetshoyv and the Jewish way of life there ceased to exist when the Nazis transported the town's Jews to the Belzec extermination camp.

Interior, Wooden synagogue in Zhydachiv

Zolochiv, Ukraine
Yiddish: Zlotshov ~ Polish: Złoczów

The first presence of Jews in Zolochiv dates to 1550, shortly after Zolochiv gained the status of a city in 1523. In 1694, Sobieski, the town's owner, permitted Jews to live everywhere in the city, trade in everything except Christian religious objects, and become artisans and enter every profession. When there was a conflict between a Jew and a Christian, the arbitrator was the owner of the town or his representative. Jews were also permitted to take part in elections to the town institutions. They were obligated to defend the town and every Jew had to keep arms and ammunition in his home.

After the First Partition of Poland, Zolochiv became part of the Austrian-Hungarian Empire until 1919 when it was returned to Poland. After World War II, Zolochiv became part of the Soviet Union. Between August and November 1942, German troops aided by Ukrainian police, sent about 4,500 Jews to the Belzec death camp where they were immediately murdered. A ghetto was established and, in April 1943 about 3,500 residents were taken to be shot in a nearby pit in the village of Yelhovitsa.

Glossary

Beit Midrash	House of study. A place set aside for study of sacred texts such as the Torah
Bimah	The pedestal on which the Torah scrolls are placed when they are being read in the synagogue
Bund	A Jewish socialist party founded in Russia in 1897. The Bund came to be devoted to Yiddish, secular Jewish nationalism, and for making a life for Jews in Europe.
Chassidim ~ Hasidism	Jewish mystical sect founded in Poland about 1750 in opposition to rationalism and ritual laxity
Cheder	A school for Jewish children in which Hebrew and religious knowledge are taught
Eretz Israel	Expression used to designate the land of Israel, as it was promised by God to the Jewish people, according to Biblical tradition
Ghetto	A walled section of a town where Jews were severely overcrowded, demoralized, worked, and starved to death. At some point the Nazis liquidated a ghetto by mass murder and/or transporting the inhabitants to killing centers or concentration camps
Haskalah	An intellectual movement among Jews of Eastern Europe in the 18th and 19th centuries that attempted to acquaint the masses with European and Hebrew languages and with secular education and culture to supplement Talmudic studies
Judenrat	A "Jewish council", it was a World War II administrative agency imposed by Nazi Germany on Jewish communities across occupied Europe
Market Town	Shtetl that held weekly markets when the peasants came to town to attend church and trade goods. They sold their surplus goods to Jewish middlemen and purchased trade goods from Jewish merchants.
Menorah	A candelabra with seven or nine lights that is used in Jewish worship
Mitnagdim	A religious movement among Eastern European Jews which resisted the rise of Hasidism
Shtetl	A small town with a substantial Jewish population, a nobleman who owned the town and peasants who worked the land.
Talmud	The Talmud is a collection of writings that covers the full gamut of Jewish law and tradition, compiled, and edited between the third and sixth centuries.
Talmud Torah	Religious school for boys of modest backgrounds, where they were given an elementary education in Hebrew, the Torah, and the Talmud.
Torah	The first five books of the Bible
Torah Ark	Ornamental chamber in the synagogue that houses the Torah scrolls
Yeshiva	An Orthodox Jewish rabbinical seminary
Yom Kippur	Day of Atonement; a day set aside for fasting, depriving oneself of pleasures, and repenting for the sins of the previous year.
Zionism	A movement for the re-establishment, development, and protection of a Jewish nation in what is now Israel.

Artist Statement

What started as the creation of a simple Jewish New Year's card has become a journey that has reinvented my life. Inspired by the wooden synagogues of Eastern Europe and their Jewish cultural history, I began to capture their images in block printing.

My artistic focus and inspiration flow from two sources: my medium, block printing, and Jewish culture and history. I love the feel of the wood or linoleum under the carving tools, which transports me to another dimension. In block printing, one must remove the surface, leaving behind the surface that will accept the ink and print. When color is added, a second block must be carved. The process of working backwards and in reverse is an enjoyable challenge.

In recent years, I studied Japanese Sumi-e and Chinese Brush Painting. Several synagogues are rendered in this style. Thus, I can work with shades of gray and a touch of color, in addition to the use of black ink.

Although the wooden synagogues and the vibrant Jewish presence in Eastern Europe became victims of the Holocaust, I hope my art evokes these beautiful structures and provides a glimpse into their glorious past.

After retiring from a career as a Social Studies and Culinary Arts teacher, my inner artist and historian emerged in 2012 when I began to make linocuts of Wooden synagogues.

Meet the Artist

Bill's first show in Poland was in the Film, Sound, and Photography Studio, and the Bialystok Opera House. The San Diego Repertory Theater used twenty of Bill's linocuts to decorate the theater for the show *"The Dybbuk for Hannah and Sam's Wedding."* The Yiddishpiel Theater of Israel used his *Lost Souls Over the Shtetl* linocut during production of *Abrham Goldfarb's The Sorceress.* Bill has presented and lectured at Florida Atlantic University, several local and international Jewish Genealogy Societies as well as many synagogues.

Bill now divides his time between Long Beach NY and Boca Raton Florida with his wife Elaine. Bill has two children and Elaine has three. They share seven grandchildren and one great grandchild.

Acknowledgements

I must begin by thanking my wife Elaine, whose inspiration made this book possible. When she introduced me to Jewish genealogy, it brought out the historian in me. She encouraged my artwork and put up with the mess I made. Reading early drafts, making suggestions, and editing helped immensely in the creation of this book. Elaine is my objective critic, my best friend, and my groupie.

I would like to acknowledge the work of several historians who provided valuable information found in their books: Maria and Kazimierz Piechotka, *"Wooden Synagogues,"* Z. Yagina, *"Wooden Synagogues: Masterpieces of Jewish Art,"* and Aiste Niunkaite-Raciuniene *"The World of Lithuanian Jewish Traditional Art and Symbols."* These works served as excellent resources and for images and information about wooden synagogues.

Thank you, Mr. Fontana, my eighth-grade printing teacher from J.H.S. 252 in Brooklyn, New York, for teaching me how to make linocuts. I also owe a debt of gratitude to my more recent art teachers Petro Punta, Irving Abramson, Denis Aufiery, Michael Chesely, Ron Garrett, and Ying Zhou.

I would like to thank Ben Lapin of Speedball, Inc., for his generosity in providing linocut supplies.

I am extremely grateful for the work of my son-in-law, Schuyler Bush of Mule Train, Inc, Web Design and Hosting, for providing a fantastic web site for me: www.billfarran.com

Many thanks to Rickie Leiter, founder, and publisher of Rickie Reports in South Florida, for her enthusiasm in promoting my art shows and work, and for being ever supportive.

Finally, I would like to express immense gratitude to Dr. Tomasz Wisniewski for being my mentor, for his friendship and encouragement, for hosting exhibitions of my work in Poland and for writing the introduction to this book.

List of Towns

Yiddish	Nation	Town	Page
Baklerove	Poland	Bakałarzewo	9
Bishenkovitz	Belarus	Byeshankovichy	37
Brizdivitz	Ukraine	Berezdivtsi	63
Dubrovno	Belarus	Dubroŭna	39
Felshtin	Ukraine	Skelivka	85
Gombin	Poland	Gabin	10
Grayding	Ukraine	Horodok	66
Grodne	Belarus	Hrodna	40
Gvozdetz	Ukraine	Gvozdets	68
Horochov	Ukraine	Horokhiv	67
Kaminka	Ukraine	Kamyanka Buzka	70
Kartoz-Brezah	Belarus	Byaroza	36
Kelm	Lithuania	Kelme	56
Khodorov	Ukraine	Khodorov	72
Kinsk	Poland	Konskie	13
Kitaigorod	Ukraine	Kitajgorod	75
Kosov Latski	Poland	Kosów Lacki	16
Kozhanhorodok	Belarus	Kažan-Haradok	41
Kurnik	Poland	Kórnik	15
Lantzekronia	Ukraine	Zarechanka	91
Lipsk	Poland	Lipsko	17
Lunna	Belarus	Lunna	42
Lutomiersk	Poland	Lutomiersk	18
Mikhalpol	Ukraine	Mychajliwha	76
Minkovitz	Ukraine	Min'kivtsi	77
Mogielnica	Poland	Mogielnica	19
Molev	Belarus	Mahilyow	43
Narovla	Belarus	Narowlya	45
Nashelsk	Poland	Nasielsk	20
Neishat	Poland	Nowe Meistro	21
Olik	Ukraine	Olyka	80
Olkenik	Lithuania	Valkininkai	60
Ozra	Belarus	Ozëry	46
Petchinizhin	Ukraine	Pechenizhyn	82
Piesk	Poland	Piaski	22
Pinsk	Belarus	Pinsk	47
Planch	Poland	Polaniec	23
Poritsk	Ukraine	Pavlivka	81
Pren	Lithuania	Prienai	57
Probishta	Ukraine	Pogrebishche	84

Yiddish	Nation	Town	Page
Pshedbozsh	Poland	Przedborz	24
Rakov	Poland	Raków	25
Shavlan	Lithuania	Siaulenai	59
Sheps	Poland	Sierpc	27
Shnodovo	Poland	Sniadowo	28
Shukian	Lithuania	Šaukėnai	58
Sidra	Poland	Sidra	26
Smotritch	Ukraine	Smotrich	87
Sobkov	Poland	Sobkow	29
Sopotkin	Belarus	Sapotskin	48
Suchavola	Poland	Suchowola	30
Talna	Ukraine	Tal'ne	88
Uzlion	Belarus	Uzlyany	49
Vashulkova	Poland	Wasilkow	32
Vileyka	Belarus	Vileyka	50
Vilkovishk	Lithuania	Vilkaviškis	61
Visoki	Poland	Wysokie Mazowieckie	33
Vitebsk	Belarus	Vitsyebsk	51
Volp	Belarus	Volpa	52
Vorke	Poland	Warka	31
Yablanov	Ukraine	Yabluniv	89
Yanov	Poland	Janów Sokolski	11
Yanov	Ukraine	Dolyna	64
Yarmolintza	Ukraine	Yarmolyntsi	90
Yartchev	Ukraine	Novyy Yarychiv	78
Yedvavna	Poland	Jedwabne	12
Yurburg	Lithuania	Jurbarkas	55
Zablodove	Poland	Zabludów	34
Zhidetshoy	Ukraine	Zhydachiv	92
Zhlodin	Belarus	Zhlodin	53
Zlotshov	Ukraine	Zolochiv	94

Book Review

Ron Garrett,
Artist and Printmaker

Genuinely a nice body of work you have created in your book. I am impressed, and many of these examples I clearly remember you developing and talking about when you took my Printmaking courses at the Boca Raton Museum of Art School nearly a decade ago. So, I know you have a passion for the subject, which really lends itself to relief carving and the expressive nature of your approach. Bill. I always noticed a sense of urgency in your prints and a need to drive ahead into the image, to get it inked and quickly printed on paper. There is a relationship to the German Expressionist artists of the 1920's and 30's in the raw, folk, and crafted style you are attracted to, and this also translates very well into depicting the many wooden architectural structures now lost to history and culture. Bravo Bill! God Speed! You have achieved everything you hope to produce in a meaningful presentation, with the scope and message many will surely be attracted to and want to share.

Ron Garrett